MW01198875

YOU M—

1930

THIS

MILESTONES, MEMORIES,
TRIVIA AND FACTS, NEWS EVENTS,
PROMINENT PERSONALITIES &
SPORTS HIGHLIGHTS OF THE YEAR

TO :

FROM :

MESSAGE :

selected and researched
by
betsy dexter

WARNER **W** TREASURES ™

PUBLISHED BY WARNER BOOKS

A TIME WARNER COMPANY

Warner Books, Inc.
1271 Avenue of the Americas
New York, New York 10020

Warner Treasures is a
trademark of Warner Books, Inc.

A Time Warner Company

DESIGN:
CAROL BOKUNIEWICZ DESIGN
PRINTED IN SINGAPORE
FIRST PRINTING: SEPTEMBER 1996
10 9 8 7 6 5 4 3 2 1
ISBN: 0-446-91142-9

As the Depression deepened, 4 million Americans found them
selves out of work and out of luck. President Herbert Hoover asked for
$100 to $150 million for public works programs. Congress responded with
$116 million for construction work, and another $45 million in drought
relief. The International Apple Shippers Association gave 6,000 jobless
men surplus apples on credit to sell on streetcorners for a nickel apiece.
2

In February, New York City began installing traffic lights at busy intersections. The decision followed complaints from drivers who claimed pedestrians strayed into the path of oncoming vehicles. The lights were developed in 1923 by Garrett A. Morgan, the African-American businessman who also invented the gas mask.

The Smoot-Hawley Tariff Bill, raising duties to an all-time high, was signed into law to combat America's sharp decline in international trade.

newsreel

THE SUPREME COURT RULED THAT BUYING BOOTLEG LIQUOR WAS NOT A VIOLATION OF THE EIGHTEENTH AMENDMENT.

BUGS MORAN

Gang warfare erupted in Chicago, when mobsters wielding machine guns burst into the swanky Fox Lake Hotel and mowed down members of the **Bugs Moran gang.**

Congress established the Veterans Administration to aid former servicemen and their dependents.

In protest against India's salt tax, **Mahatma Gandhi** led Indians on a 200-mile march to the sea to obtain salt. He was arrested and imprisoned without trial. It was the boldest act of civil disobedience yet by the slight, charismatic leader in his campaign to end British rule.

headlines

international

The Turkish city of Constantinople was officially renamed Istanbul.

In Ethiopia, Ras Tafari changed his name and became Emperor Haile Selassie.

Hitler's Nazi Party emerged as the majority party in the German national elections, winning 107 seats in the governing body, the Reichstag.

The fad of "tree sitting" swept the nation.

For The First Time *Anywhere!*

The most revolutionary idea in the history of food will be revealed in Springfield today

BIRDS EYE FROSTED FOODS

Frozen food, processed by Brooklyn, NY, native Clarence Birdseye, hit the commercial market for the first time on March 6.

'30

Astronomer Clyde W. Tombaugh, of Illinois, discovered the ninth planet. He named it Pluto.

PAINTER GRANT WOOD COMPLETED HIS MOST FAMOUS WORK, *AMERICAN GOTHIC.*

6

Despite the fact that **Prohibition** celebrated its tenth anniversary, alcoholism soared. Hospitals and insurance companies reported that deaths from alcoholism were now six times as common as they were a decade ago. Dry law opponents claimed that the law had spawned graft and murder, enriching bootleggers and hoodlums. "Because of Prohibition," claimed officials of the Moderation League, "a spirit of revolt is abroad in the nation."

Amelia Earhart set a world aviation record for women, flying 171 miles per hour in a Lockheed Vega.

Vannevar Bush, an electrical engineer, developed a differential analyzer, the world's first analog computer.

cultural
milestones

By the end of the year, more than 1,300 banks had closed their doors.

"AMOS 'N' ANDY

radio

Lowell Thomas became known for his trademark sign-off, "So long until tomorrow!" Another comedy crowd-pleaser, "The Cuckoo Hour," kept America in stitches with this wacky bit of badinage: "There will be a brief pause while we throw at you Mrs. Pennyfeather's Personal Service for Perturbed People."

premieres

"Lum and Abner," starring Chester Lauck and Norris Goff

"Singin' Sam, the Barbasol Man," with Harry Frankel

"Town Crier," Alexander Woollcott's mix of gossip and literature

"Believe It or Not," hosted by Robert Ripley

"Walter Winchell"

"Death Valley Days," starring Tim Frawley

ROBERT RIPLEY (R)
AND OZZIE NELSON

9

LON CHANEY

D E A T H S

Lon Chaney, Hollywood's legendary "Man of a Thousand Faces" and star of *Hunchback of Notre Dame,* died August 26 in Los Angeles, CA.

Sir Arthur Conan Doyle, the father of Sherlock Holmes, died in Crowborough, England, July 7.

William Howard Taft, the 27th U.S. president, died in Washington, DC, March 8.

Herbert Dow, founder of the Dow Chemical Company, died October 15.

D. H. Lawrence, British author best known for his banned novel *Lady Chatterley's Lover,* died March 2 in France.

Henry Clay Folger, American philanthropist who developed the world's first Shakespeare collection, the Folger Shakespeare Library, died in New York June 11.

Fridtjof Nansen, the Norwegian explorer who led the first expedition across the ice fields of Greenland and won the Nobel Peace Prize for refugee work, died May 30.

celeb births

CLINT EASTWOOD, actor, director, and mayor of Carmel, CA, was born May 31 in San Francisco, CA.

ASTRONAUT NEIL ARMSTRONG, first man to walk on the moon, was born August 5 in Wapakoneta, OH.

SEAN CONNERY, the original James Bond, was born in Edinburgh, Scotland, August 25.

SANDRA DAY O'CONNOR, first woman justice of the Supreme Court, was born March 26 in El Paso, TX.

celeb weddings

Doris Doscher, model pictured on the 1930 U.S. quarter, married **Dr. Wilhelm Baum**, a psychiatrist at the Jewish Institute of Religion in Manhattan.

Margot Einstein, sculptress and daughter of genius Albert Einstein, married Dr. Dmitri Marianov, a Russian scientist and writer.

Ugo Zacchini, 31, world-renowned "Human Cannonball" in Ringling Brothers Barnum & Bailey Circus, married Berlin performer **Elizabeth Walker**. The groom made a spectacular entrance.

milestones

1. **chant of the jungle** Roy Ingraham
2. **the man from the south** Ted Weems
3. **happy days are here again** Benny Meroff
4. **puttin' on the ritz** Harry Richman
5. **happy days are here again** Ben Selvin
6. **stein song (university of maine)** Rudy Vallee
7. **when it's springtime in the rockies** Hilo Hawaiian Orchestra
8. **when it's springtime in the rockies** Ben Selvin
9. **dancing with tears in my eyes** Rudy Vallee
10. **little white lies** Guy Lombardo

30 hit music

Fats Waller, hot off his 1929 Broadway smash *Hot Chocolates,* scored a hit with the show tune for "Ain't Misbehavin'." Beneath the plump comic facade, critics said, there lurked the lean soul of a brilliant pianist and composer. Fats wowed the audience with his action on "the mothbox," pet name for his beloved organ.

Broadway gave the nation two more hits with the Gershwin brothers' *Girl Crazy,* which included the popular tunes "I Got Rhythm" and "Embraceable You."

Lionel Hampton and Louis Armstrong made their first recording together.

GERSHWINS

fiction

The Pulitzer Prize went to Edna Ferber's bestseller, *Cimarron*, a story of pioneer Oklahoma.

Private eye Sam Spade made his way onto the literary scene this year, with the release of Dashiell Hammett's *The Maltese Falcon*.

14

books

It was 49 homers for Babe Ruth this year. The Babe's salary reached a record 80 grand, more than the president's.

In baseball, Philadelphia took the World Series, defeating the National League's St. Louis four games to three. Philly's Al Simmons clinched the American League batting title with .380, while New York's Bill Terry took the National League title with a whopping .401.

Mildred "Babe" Didrikson won her first national honors at an AAU meet in Dallas. Her javelin and baseball throws earned her first-place titles, and her second-place long jump bettered a world record. Her nickname came from her ability to hit a baseball like her idol, Babe Ruth.

IN AUTO RACING, BILLY ARNOLD TOOK THE 18TH ANNUAL INDY 500 AT 100.5 MPH IN A MILLER HARTZ SPECIAL RACER.

Jockey Earl Sande rode Gallant Fox to the Triple Crown.

sports

Max Schmeling won the heavyweight boxing title from Jack Sharkey. He took the bout on a foul. 75,000 attended the match.

Amateur BOBBY JONES retired after achieving the Grand Slam of golf by winning the British Open, British Amateur, U.S. Open, and U.S. Amateur tournaments.

MARLENE DIETRICH

academy awards

All Quiet on the Western Front snagged two Oscars, Best Picture and Best Director, for **Lewis Milestone**. Actor **George Arliss** competed against himself for Best Actor. His performance in *Disraeli* took the statue, beating out his performance in *The Green Goddess*. **Norma Shearer** won Best Actress for *The Divorcee*. And in a Hollywood rarity, female screenwriter **Frances Marion** won an Oscar for *The Big House*, a prison movie.

Two foreign beauties made debuts this year. **Greta Garbo** appeared in *Anna Christie*, her first talkie. The legend's first words on screen were uttered in her husky, alluring Swedish accent: "Gif me a visky with ginger ale on the side. And don't be stingy, baby." **Marlene Dietrich**, dubbed the German Garbo, was brought to the United States by director Josef von Sternberg. She starred in the darkly erotic film *The Blue Angel*, in which she played a cruel and beautiful chorus girl, Lola-Lola.

movies

ACTOR JOHN BARRYMORE PLAYED HERMAN MELVILLE'S EPIC CHARACTER CAPTAIN AHAB WITH HAMLET-LIKE FLOURISH IN DIRECTOR LLOYD BACON'S ADAPTATION OF *MOBY-DICK*.

GRETA GARBO

Depression-era suffering proved a boon to theater owners, who packed in a weekly average of 90 million moviegoers looking for escape from their workaday woes.

20

-30

Confusion reigned in the price department as new models were shown at the National Automobile Show. Four makes had a higher price tag, while five other lines reduced prices.

cars

CAR RADIOS MADE THEIR APPEARANCE THIS YEAR. CADILLAC, CHRYSLER, DODGE, LASALLE, MARMON, AND ROOSEVELT CARS WERE WIRED FOR RADIO INSTALLATION—AS WERE ALL POLICE CARS.

Cadillac introduced its V16. Dubbed "the land yacht" by its manufacturer, the Great Gatsby–era vehicle was designed as the ultimate luxury car. Its 452- cubic- inch motor developed 165 horsepower, and could make an incredible 90 miles per hour. A grand total of 3,250 wealthy buyers snapped them up for their own Depression driving pleasure.

The Depression caused a sharp drop in automobile sales, and many small manufacturers were forced out of business.

This year's fashion silhouettes were slim and tall. The look featured streamlined hips and big shoulders. The big bosom was out; small was in. Skirts were longer than the previous spring, reaching midway between knee and ankle. Some afternoon and evening dresses were ankle-length.

Chanel's collection was the success of the season. She showed evening gowns that were "picturesque, fanciful and feminine."

fashion

In hairdressing, gone were the Bob and the Eton Crop, replaced by smoothly waved hair and tiny curls.

Magnifying mirrors became part of the modern woman's makeup kit this year. They were needed to help pencil in eyebrows—always well-plucked—along with applying black mascara and eye shadow.

The angular look was featured in makeup.

The latest hats

were described in lyrical prose as having been "brought down from heaven on an angel's wing . . . inspired by poets . . . created by some wondrous Djinn. . . ." Head-hugging, with a narrow, rolled-back brim, these hats were designed to flatter, provoke, and allure.

In 1930, the **Pepsi-Cola Company** was busy trying to compete with the Coca-Cola Company. Pepsi came out with a larger 12-ounce bottle. The cost was a nickel, the same price as Coke's 6-ounce bottle.

final factoid

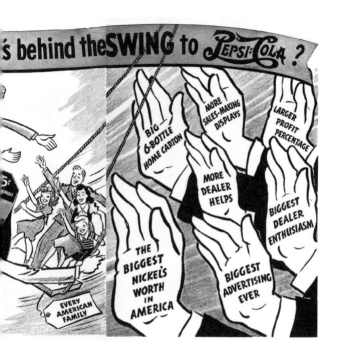

archive photos: inside front cover, pages 1, 2, inside back cover

associated press: pages 3, 4, 5, 7, 16, 17

photofest: pages 8, 9, 10, 13, 18, 19, 23

ewing galloway: page 15

gaslight: pages 6, 20, 25

photo research:
alice albert

coordination:
rustyn birch

design:
carol bokuniewicz design
paul ritter